The Ruined Motel

The Houghton Mifflin New Poetry Series

Judith Leet, *Pleasure Seeker's Guide*
David St. John, *Hush*
Heather McHugh, *Dangers*
Gerald Stern, *Lucky Life*
Judith Wright, *The Double Tree: Selected Poems 1942–1976*
Christopher Bursk, *Standing Watch*
Thomas Lux, *Sunday*
James McMichael, *Four Good Things*
Reginald Gibbons, *The Ruined Motel*

Also by Reginald Gibbons

Roofs, Voices, Roads: Poems
The Poet's Work, editor
Selected Poems of Luis Cernuda, translator
Guillén on Guillén, translator, with A. L. Geist

The
Ruined Motel

P O E M S

Reginald Gibbons

Houghton Mifflin Company   Boston   1981

Library of Congress Cataloging in Publication Data

Gibbons, Reginald.
   The ruined motel.

(Houghton Mifflin new poetry series)
   I. Title. II. Series.
PS3557.I1392R8   811'.54   81-6415
ISBN 0-395-31659-6   AACR2
ISBN 0-395-31660-X (pbk.)

Printed in the United States of America

W 10 9 8 7 6 5 4 3 2 1

Acknowledgments

I wish to thank the editors of the following magazines for publishing some of the poems in this book. In several instances, the poems have been changed since their first publication.

American Poetry Review: "Breath," "We Say," "The Ruined Motel."
Atlantic Monthly: "Hoppy."
Canto: "First We Will Make a List."
The Hudson Review: "Michael's Room."
Inquiry Magazine: "The Voice of Someone Else," "Wood."
The New Republic: " 'Luckies.' "
Occident: "The Days," "For My Daughter."
The Paris Review: "At Noon," "The Cedar River."
Quest/81: Part 1 of "This Morning."
The Sewanee Review: "The Letter."
Stand: "Small Elegy."
University Magazine: "At the Temple of Asklepios on Kos."
Part 3 of "At Latitude Thirty" was published in *Occident;* Part 4 in *The Iowa Review;* Part 5 in *The Ontario Review.*
"Those Who Are Gone" was first published as a broadside by Palaemon Press, Ltd., 1980.
"This Morning" was first published in a limited edition by Eleutherian Printers, 1981.

for Gail
for Gary
for Elaine

Contents

In
the Kingdom

In the Kingdom

The lamb's head was caught,
it had butted its way
at the squared fence-wire
till it pushed through
and was held. We thought
for a moment, remembering edgy courtesies
when we had trespassed before.

This was where the wind and a stream
had hidden a little valley,
and one farm, at the foot of steep
pastures, lay in the deep fold.
We had seen the hills and fields
tilt, as we walked, into a green
perfection, and when we'd looked up

we'd tripped in mid-air —
watched a hawk come
leap the crest above us with
two wingbeats and whistle
over the sheep, floating level
with our eyes as the coomb
dropped away deeper and broader.

The hawk scanned the hillsides
and near us in a small grove
starlings crackled like lighted tinder.
Invisible as angels, we waited —
a toy man and dog moved
from house to barn, and cattle under
a mossy roof called for milking.

And there before us was
the lamb — tugging at its own head
in jerks, snared inside
its field by a blind five-yard
fence-spur near the gate.
The ewe stood at a distance, answering
the high bleats, marble-eyed.

I called out and waved to the man
who didn't see or hear me.
Then I climbed in, the ewe
balked and dodged away as I took hold
of the lamb, which leapt with fear
till I could push the ears down
and with a hard shove back the head through.

It staggered and fell,
tottered up, ran off and banged
into the ewe. It pulled at a teat
but was led straight down to the flock,
all of them jumpy and dull.
I came back over the gate
and you took my arm in yours.

As if loosed from a tether
the hawk rose then, cupped a gust
in its wings and banked, slipped over
the far hill, following a hedge.
The farm tucked itself further
into its fold with each step
we took toward the village

and disappeared behind us when
the lane turned, cut the slope,
under sparse elms, and sank a foot more
into the red earth. Then came the schoolyard,
the little houses, gradients
marking the descent, each roofline
lower than the one before.

And our door, that led
into a happy solitude that year.
Looking at the map, we talked of the stream
called Healeyes, and the place whose name
meant "a muddy ford." Reg, you said
much later, when we were quiet,
What was it like to touch the lamb's head?

At
Latitude Thirty

The Voice of Someone Else

I've lived under this big porch a long time.
Where you are — where you breathe
and talk and things come to hand —
is above me: warmth, painted wood, prospects . . .
But I like this lattice-shadow better.
(You may remember now, with a chill,
how you caught a glimpse of my eye
on you, from in here, but it doesn't matter
what you think you saw in the checkered light —
fine skin and jewels, or a curved beak,
or fur, or scales that rustled as they disappeared.)

I am my own keeper. I have lost nothing.
Every old thing is with me — the afternoon
when the field burned, and the good belt
with the turquoise buckle, and the long game
under the lights . . .
But also the stories that your sister told
her friend when no living thing was listening.

When I come up, it is by a passage
inside you, to look out through
your eyes, that are mine any time I want.
Likewise your body, likewise your soul.
The things that rouse me?
Hurt, strength, good weather, bad weather,
accidents, secrets being told, secrets
held back, and then, knowing —
this comes from far off, calling me from above —
that the hand is holding a pen.

for William Goyen

Today

The sunlight showed only as a glow
in the threads of the window curtains.
Daddy called us to get up,
we gathered our clothes and cold shoes
and ran to dress in the kitchen,
where all four burners on the Chambers range
were torching the air with clean
flame. Frank Blair read the news;
the camera caught New Yorkers on their way
to work in the snow, waving through
the glass or holding up signs,
"J.F.K. for President" and "Betty
in Houston — Happy Birthday."
                                    But whoever
she was, had she seen it? We told
the others outside about Betty, and threw
a last rock or two into the ditch
before getting on the yellow bus.
It left Tinker alone by the road.
He waited for the special van,
and we had teased him till he cried,
tongue-tied and cold, and hid
his hearing aid with one hand
over his ear. Out the back, we
watched him follow the bus a few steps
and then give us the finger.

I don't care about Kennedy
any more, or the message that
was lost or the way people dressed

then and thought that television
could amuse and be useful, or
how hard it was to get up early
and behave. I want to know what
happened in Tinker's years after the sun
blazed through clouds and spotlit his rage.

Breath

I remember coming up,
pushing off from the bottom
through dull ringing silence
toward the undersurface of the water
where light sparkled — or patterns
fanned across the roof-fabric:
that deep comfort, long ago, of
being carried to the house
in the dark, half-asleep, only
half-interrupting the dreams
that had made the car a craft
among stars. But the air —
and the house — held
depths too, where someone else,
someone larger, locked the doors,
did late-night chores and turned out
the lights, too tired now
to stop the inevitable
fight, rising to it . . .

Underwater, you hear bodies
burble over you, smashing the sunlight —
and voices in other rooms begin
to swell, drawers shutting, bags
slammed down from closet shelves,
footsteps . . . Till a child's fear,
held under, shudders free, floating up
to explode with a gasp, and splashes
out of sleep, and sucks air,
and discovers that nothing
consoles, there is no air,
there is no waking, not anywhere.

First We Will Make a List

It was not a tin-roofed barn
nor straight furrows in fields
cleared of pines, nor the sooty face
and the empty lunchbox at six,
nor grease under the nails and a temper,
nor the soft belly without
its desk-armor every night, nor
the long line coiled to a perfect
cone with baited hooks,
nor pink blooms jammed in a close bouquet.
It was a panel truck, Aqua-Velva,
United Commercial Travelers, a string tie,
cash, and I would ride along
to all the Chinese grocers, dirt road
corner shanty stores, country
butchers and venison sausage processors
till we finally decided what
I would be and how you would like it.

The Days

Up first, alone, only you
caught the earth dipping
just before dawn into silence.
The cars waiting outside
glistened in the dark with dew.
Then a mockingbird would go back
to the song it would break with a buzz,
and through the walls you'd hear
a few early workers, taking
the shortcut down our street,
gun it coming out of the S-
curve and leap into third for
the straight quarter mile to the stoplight.

Pulling the door shut behind you
at six, by yourself on the porch,
you left us still asleep to fall
with the weight of the day
toward bottom, where we'd come
in late from an aimless, hours-long
cruise in the Fairlane and go softly by
your bed at midnight to the bathroom.
In a scratchy chatter two commentators
would be tallying late-season
farm-team hits and runs
from the floodlit stillness
of Busch Stadium. Then came
the studio insomniac's voice —
that all-night call-in debate on divorce,
gun control, drinking . . .
till the produce and livestock prices
came on at five and you were up.

"Luckies"

The loop of rusty cable incises
its shadow on the stucco wall.
My father smiles shyly and takes
one of my cigarettes, holding it

awkwardly at first, as if it were
a dart, while the yard slowly
swings across the wide sill of daylight.
Then it is a young man's quick hand

that rises to his lips, he leans against the wall,
his white shirt open at the throat,
where the skin is weathered, and he chats
and daydreams, something he never does.

Smoking his cigarette, he is even
younger than I am, a brother who
begins to guess, amazed, that what
he will do will turn out to be this.

He recalls the house he had
when I was born, leaning against it
now after work, the pale stucco
of memory, 1947.

Baby bottles stand near the sink inside.
The new wire of the telephone, dozing
in a coil, waits for the first call.
The years are smoke.

We Say

We say a heart breaks — like
a stick, maybe, or a bottle
or a wave. But it seems
more like the field clump
that crackles upward from a match
and collapses, grass filaments
sparking in the ash-dust
then going out. Today
I take myself down by steps,
one at a time, into the sadness
I admit I can't always reach.
There should be a room
at the bottom of the black stairway,
my friends sitting with strangers,
waiting, but there's no one,
only the memory, when
the pale air flickers as if
it were an invisible flame,
of my aunt in her hospital bed
and beside her, about to be left
alone — the last sister, and so soon —
my mother, bent over
the purse in her lap, eyes closed.
I can see the patent leather gloss
and the shiny clasp that until
just now she had been
snapping open and shut, till —
just now — it broke. That breaking —
like a voice that cracks, cursing
or crying, or the song that falls,

out of thinking too far ahead,
into a smouldering loneliness —
was that the sound of the heart?

Michael's Room

Your hand in your grandfather's —
as though the bone just beneath the skin
had cleared his thin flesh
and called out the skeletal glow
in your own fingers, too soon.
Bone against bone, surprising you,
bruises you both with dread.
Morphine, stitched incisions, nausea —
and your father sits in a chair,
his hands on his knees, still
brooding on the blood that made him faint.
While you wait now, holding yourself
together with the hurting that threads
its way through you, cold and hot.

A neighbor has brought her preacher.
"May we say a prayer over you, son?"
An unreasonable hope clarifies
their own cloudy pain, and his voice
climbs into a high monotone, as if
he were speaking to someone who's far off
or deaf or . . . Your grandfather?
He's not really here.
He's been banished for good by your mother,
who blames him for the wreck.
Everything he's ever done . . . Everything
you might have. But he hovers
in your dream of waking up healed
and you stare at his hand holding yours.

Lentils

Ezra Pound again

You still appear
to test me, interrupting
the line and knocking
it apart — though I can't
be sure it's you.
From so far off, coming at me
out of books and other people's mouths
you're far less real than
the old woman from Łodz
who forgot who I was
when she was eighty,
I fifteen.

Your silence, and hers.
Your madness, that was
not charming, not fruitful.
And hers, her fear:
her speechless thorazine stare
as, on some inner screen
that she thought
sheltered her from us
who had loved her,
she watched the steady
image of some one thing
she could remember — perhaps as you
in the Washington asylum
had thought of the paper clips
rusting in your desk at Rapallo.

When she spoke to herself
did she say we didn't love her?
She could tell.

So she still appears to me, still strong,
to test me, scolding and correcting —
posture, English, piano.
The faint faint accent and scent of age,
and on the stove behind her —
forgotten for the moment —
the steaming pot of lentils.
No, no. Try it again.

The Letter

A scene remembered: the car
stopping, a back door opens, four
figures slowly climb down in the dark,

too frightened to speak, put out
as a punishment, and the damp night
finally shuts us up
like a chill hand slapped over
our bickering and complaints.

We held on to each other, our backs
to an infinite black canebrake —
a forlorn little circle — and whimpered
as the tires scuffed through
soft dust and rumbled away.

Then nothing . . .
The drone and flutter and deafening throb
of the world, one small light
burning far away atop a derrick.
We had no hopes,

could barely draw breath to sob
till the car crept up again,
headlights off. No one of us would
break the grip of another to get in.

And I tell myself: we have
a pact, ever since, never to let go.
But that timid dance, hands
locked in passionate fear,
ends today with a letter: "One

curious thing. I remember the horror
of being driven away in the car while you
alone . . ."

So I look at my hands. They are empty,
and the cane thicket whispers in the wind.
When the car comes back, the ten-year-old boy —
the oldest — talky, thin, vain, wanting
too soon to reason and argue, will look in
at the startled man and woman,
the three children, and turn away,
a stranger of thirty, unable to speak.

When the car comes back.

At Latitude Thirty

1. At Lat. 30°

Rub my legs, please rub my legs, they hurt.
Your hands are warm.

If there's a spider under my bed
or if someone tries to come in the window

will you help me? I didn't mean
to hurt my sisters — and burning the field

was an accident. It's going to storm — we'll
unplug everything and sit together

on the floor, it's so hot,
the air smells like rain and dirt . . .

Then the clouds would creak like leather
and the light broke — the sky

split open along a seam and gleamed
through the crack, and showed us

summer's suffering, a turmoil
of horned toads and hospitals, the streets

that memory depopulates till
the dust on hot fenders speaks louder

than any living thing.
                        Wake up, wake up —
Daddy has your breakfast on the table.

2. Brother

Through the green glass of that daylight,
all things out of shape, I remember:

seven cedar fence-poles from the gate,
dig in the cakey white soil where we

buried our treasure in a coffee can . . .
And after rain the sun would burn

back down even harder, and we would
leave our hiding place and weave

home through steam-swaddled saplings,
high sparse brush, slack barbed wire.

But we forgot what we had put there
and could think of nothing we loved

that was missing. Forgot our bodies
and took new ones. Was it the seventh fence-post?

The bare-ribbed field still awaits the probing
grit-shiny steel of a spade.

* * *

Its malevolent little eye blinked
and your face erupted in blood.

We screamed, then laughed. It was true.
But stroke the belly softly, head

to tail down the fine white scales,
and it sleeps. With a string

tied around its neck, behind the horns,
and the other end to a shirt-button,

it would sit placidly on a shoulder
all day, doze and disdain food

till you dropped it
back into the anonymous white dust.

⸱⸱⸱

I had not thought of the rule,
I had simply followed it:

and with the warm shell in the chamber, smoking
as the silence held our lungs in its fist,

and a hole in the wall that could have been
your body, I slowly lowered

the four-ten. That close.
So all the rules were right.

⸱⸱⸱

After the near miss;
after play in the willow-ditches;

after exclusions and slights;
after giving up the chase

to let what scurried away from us
escape with its own life;

after the raging, bitter fights,
when the wrestled standstill finally

turned to a tired embrace, with all
of the enmity but that which had scarred us

thrown aside forever: there remained
the doomed quest, the hopeless task.

How will you get rid of me,
my dear one? Ahead of you in the train

of the years, the trek across
plains of Texas decades, I couldn't help

stealing some of your thunder, jolted
ahead as I was in my own lumbering course.

And I took each day of our lives
and placed it on your shoulders —

the act that is my crime, and my hope.

3. Mother's Room, 1963

Archaic concession to the automobile,
the Buffalo Speedway

curves past the sandstone
façade, small snake and staff

over the doorway. In the lot, the parked
car is running but we're not in it yet.

We stand nearby looking up at
the third floor, counting the unopened windows

until we reach the twelfth, and then
we can make you out despite

the reflected sun-blaze that
wobbles with our heartbeats in the glass.

You wave a handkerchief, white blur
in the grim honey-yellow walls,

and around you in the tiny room,
stacked on the nightstand and ranged

along the sill, the popsicle-stick products
of an intense will to stay sane, to kill

the loneliness till your lungs
heal. In the car, in traffic, we return

to the lives that have become merely ours.

4. The Homecoming

This summer the garden really did make.

The mildly toxic tapwater
percolates at a boil through string beans.

Bread and salad on the table,
the knives and forks that never have changed.

As I walked past the closet doors
they swung open like vaults

and displayed the artifacts
of an earlier self, stacked neatly,

but for a journey
I made without them: I wanted

nothing with me, and one day
I will have to pay a stranger to return

to all this archaeology and sell it.
Nothing,

in fact, is ever thrown away, but still
a ceaseless devotion to creditors has

kept the gods of income and expenditure
hovering at the windows: they

exacted a sacrifice, once, through the junkie
who appeared brandishing a gun and

(even here, in the deputized shade, under
dripping, subtropical eaves)

demanded the forgotten hopes
glittering on your ring fingers, and the key

to the car . . .

Your grandmother would like you to call her.

The trip there
leads to the realm of the fabulous —

the ribboning scissortails
pose a last time on the wires;

new apartments rise haunch-first, half-
timbering faked over plywood; and the glowing malls

whose werwolves of commerce
thrive on a diet of credit. But — attend

to the unremembered and the old:
"Drive Friendly" past buzzards standing

glutted at the roadside; fetch groceries
from the U-tote-M; heed the factory roar

transmitted through anesthetizing
airconditioners to every den . . .

As we eat, eponymous heroes haunt
newscasts and conversation: Travis,

Houston, Polk, San Felipe — streets
where trucks collide

with a televised whisper and an occasional
building crumples in flames.

Lethargic thoughts acquiesce
as anchormen recite today's crime report:

Homicides 7, Robberies 61, Assaults 29, Rapes 11
Double this sum, multiply by nine

Walk thrice in a circle. There is
a decorum that demands one's silence.

Don't you want more gravy?

This road leading home — through the security
check, jet din, past concrete fields,

yaupons and banana fronds, to this
fiefdom of regret, dotted

with petite tract castles — ends in an
old routine, the clearing away, the ritual

refusal that greets an offer
to wash the dishes. The closet doors swing

shut. There is a decorum. Put out
the light, let love fill the dark.

5. The Dream of Mississippi

At the edge of the thicket
you hesitate and I lead

the way in. After a long walk
we sit for a while on a log

and suck at the canteen,
watch a big rattler slide across the trail.

You smile at my fear, memory breathes
on the gray coals in you and they glow red.

Is this the way? I ask.
You nod and point deeper into the trees

along a sandy path you knew as a boy.
You appear as a boy,

a hot rain is falling, you chew pine resin,
your eyes grow darker, your muddy hopes

boil away in the summer sun.
You take a photograph from your pocket

and we enter it: now you are a baby
in your father's arms, you wait

to be put back down on the porch
of the new house, where behind the railing

other faces peek at the lens —
your cousins, soon to find

you their favorite, much-used toy.
The stifling light

of the sepia print is dripping
from the trees around us, sieved through

pines, sinking into
the musky earth. It is time to go on.

Through thigh-stinging underbrush I
break the old trail open,

heading for the house and artesian well.
Beside a stump, your father appears, and he

argues with his father, it is 1910, he wants
a place of his own, and the old man stands

where his own father stood before this story's time
and he sees himself in his son now and cedes him

some land. They build the house,
your father picks you up,

an itinerant photographer produces this
memento . . . You pocket it again and point

a new direction, while around us
the gatekeepers lie, jewels

glittering along their serpentine spines,
black heads yawning

with a hiss, needles ready
in a bed of clean cotton: you are twelve still,

you stub a bare toe
hunting squirrels with a sling;

for a while you hold your eyes
on the trees, then in pain

you return to that place to see
nearly buried in the road's white dust

the thick dozing body whose fangs
you had taken for a thorn.

Your mother appears, she says you
are not to run, but to walk home.

They cut you with a razor, put
your foot in a bucket of kerosene,

a week passes, and then her young
half-Indian features fade

as, ever softer, she sings
you to sleep in a rocker . . .

The doves, their calls muffled
in the heat, pass out of our hearing now.

We come into the clearing, I step away
to let you be the first to see again

after fifty years the first place
you knew. Blackberry, high weeds

and a crab-apple tree rise
where the well might be.

Beyond that, in ragged scrub,
the ruin sags, two sharp-toothed window-frames

smashed at the chimney's ankles,
bubbly glass and brick, a heap of rubbish

surrounded by thick stands of stubby pines.
You stop and I stand beside you.

Now, as I begin to cry, you speak.

6. *Begin Again*

This is none of this true.
What was true was less

and worse, what is true now
is still unfinished and will

come, like a whipping, too late
yet with a kind of love.

How could I turn these things
to words, and rouse a hurt

in you greater than anything
by saying them?

It is like a soothing, done
with love and yet too late.

This
Morning

for V. H. G.

1.

I draw the unlit room toward me,
from the deep window sill
stacked with music, past the long
side of the piano and the stilled
pyramidal metronome, past
the couch that dims the air with wood
and red wool, past small
rough gloves left muddy on the floor
near boots on open newspaper,
past the little pine's glossy silence,
through the frame of the open door,
across the table top and this page
into my empty, upended coffee glass.
I put the glass down. The room
remains, shadowed and cool.
Nothing changes, but everything
floats with me into the minutes,
still, still. Till I move.
It was for this I loosened
my grip on yesterday and let it go.

2.

The moment seems to offer us its hand.
It comes closer, as if wading this way
through high grass, and then it passes
as if it had not seen us at all.
Stay with us a little while, we say.
The field dissolves back into walls,
this room, photos of brother,
father and mother, sisters, wife.
We all talk at once, but there was never
a moment like that, when all that's
happened has been good, and nothing
bad can happen. *Stay with us
a little while,* each of us hears
all the others say, as one by one
we must leave, and each puts a hand
to another's cheek. The voices dissolve
into a silence, a realm of mute things
we have signed with our touch,
things that give me back the names I love.
I draw the unlit room toward me.

3.

I thought it was the pine tree
outside my window that had come
with me through these years.
And the desk where I read,
ate, wrote. I thought the path
unrolled before me, that when I turned
this way, not knowing I had turned,
it was this work I had set myself toward.
But it was not these things
I use or possess, flecks on a flood-sweep,
that said to me, *You may go till your care
brings you back to us*; that grew with me
as pulse-beats matching mine, however
far away; that took a living shape, like
the face that changes with my face,
beside me for as long as we last.
I see loss coming — crossing
the street to meet me, or wading
this way through the rising waters
ahead, ready to take my hand.

4.

The plummet-speed I will
ride down someday, holding tight
& tumbling away from myself
through a pale-branched darkness . . .
Falling, when the blood that is itself
a thought begins to blacken, and all
my powers black out, will I find
another power? This dim cloudy day's
the day when the city grid snaps —
a line gone down under a treelimb —
and the house darkens: clocks
stop and the refrigerator stops,
the electric coffeepot stops.
Then I hear the shy summer thrush
that has come out of the park woods
to sing and sing, while everything else
is quiet, and we sit still, waiting.
Flute-notes and trills from the sifting top
of the pine tree that stands,
as if thinking, outside my window.

5.

Let yesterday go. I let go
of it when my hands had to open
because of what came
to them out of my future
asking to be held: the faces
of those whom I love most
and will most neglect; one by one
all the things I will slight;
like water poured for me
into my cupped hands, the time
that will fall away unused
till I can take only what little
is left; the bad against which
I will have kept no vigil.
Come afterward, then, strength;
come, touch that will break like foam
above the wave of pain; words
someone will speak unbidden to soothe
all loss; rope and handle of the plummet-
speed I will ride down forever.

The
Ruined Motel

Small Elegy

Someone has left us now
before we have even touched hands.

Getting lost in the pity of it
sweeps you into an unknown stretch
of canyon where oars thud
against rock and rip free, you clutch
at help, and even though
you save yourself, the river
funnels through the gorge
and roars, roars, roars.
Regret, a backwash of pain,
one lost life swirls down rapids,
rushes away, out of reach.

It's not forgetting that you want —
it would be easy to drop
one shoulder and dive, to come up
gasping in a car on the way to work
or blue in the face over the dishpan
staring for who knows how long
at a cup scoured clean under the suds.
And not remembering.

But the absence that is born
must live as long as a man or a woman.
There: it comes invisible headfirst,
a bloodstreaked nothing, and is flushed away.
While in the white room the dry light
is cold; and waiting to be taken home
mute ghosts lie in a row of empty cribs.

For My Daughter

1.

I hear your friends in the street;
the day is as still as this room.
Speaking a nickname will turn
a head or raise an answering arm.

Why did you come in? To watch me
at my silent work? Why does
every image of you, however
hair-raising your narrow escapes,

however sulky your thwarted
afternoons, end in this pose? —
you watching me from the doorway
as I sit at my desk, finding the right phrase.

If you put your small hand to my neck
the touch chills. And even before
I look back at you, you begin
to vanish, the walls seem to come clear

through you, the photos and bookshelves
distracting me from you, myself
a distraction. And if you still
do not exist, it's because you never will.

2. (Alternatives)

. . . in the mudslide;
You died when the shack set on fire —
    two rooms, the polished bones of gray planks —
    collapsed in a glowing heap;
You died at the weaving machine
    slumped against the shiny levers,
    your lungs crinkling with nylon dust;
You died after almost escaping the pack of dogs;
You died in the kitchen with your own father's
    bullet in you, your hands raised;
You died with the gang-joke of old rope
    around your throat in the schoolyard;
You died in the infant ward with your mother's
    drugs soaked through your bain
    and your feet and arms lost on the way here;
You died under the weight of the executed townsmen;
You died with your heart wobbling till it burst,
    and the boys walking away, leaving you in the ditch;
You died . . .

3.

Blood clouds the vision: a shape
flickering through the trees
just out of sight, a sheerness,
vapor-thin, trying to appear.

No, vision clouds because there's
nothing to see: the eye strains
till it blurs with tears: a missing date,
a failed prophecy, a mistake.

This sudden urge to turn up the hill street,
taking the long way past the redbud
and dogwood — faint purple haze against
a cloud of white — was it a voice, your voice?

X-Ray Movie

One short, stooped, with bowed legs,
the other tall and quick-moving,
they sit down jerkily on dim chairs,
their teeth grip an invisible
sustenance speared with stark forks,
the plates hover with the glasses.
Mandibles, and the long long
fingers curved arthritically without
tense flesh around them,
and the faint, slipping guts . . .

They are free of what we endure, then —
there they sit in the other world,
eating while they listen
to the lost movements of Mozart's
night-music, and watch the Sioux ghost-dance,
and if they wished to make
the trip maybe they
could see the Parthenon new
or rattle their digits against
those of Jesus.

They must find this amusing —
the eyeless skulls incline
toward one another, and the shoulders
jump, jaws open now and shut with what
might be laughter, yes
the heads somehow toss themselves back
happily or is it a kind of torture —
No: in baggy gabardine, with a look

of anxious haste, the tall man emerges
from behind the lead curtains
unharmed, and the idiot's
myopic eyes and fat cheeks, as he puts
his arm in his father's, wrinkle
with a smile and he clumps out of the rays
re-embodied, wearing his suit and tie.

Wood

A cylinder of maple
set in place, feet spread apart —
and the heavy maul, fat as a hammer
but honed like an axe, draws
a semicircle overhead and strikes
through the two new halves
to leave the steel head sunk
a half-inch in the block and the ash
handle rigid in the air.
A smack of the palm, gripping as it hits
the butt end, and the blade
rolls out of the cut. The half-logs
are still rocking on the flagstones.

So much less than what we have been
persuaded to dream, this necessity for wood
might have sufficed, but it is what
we have been taught to disown and forget.
Yet just such hardship is what saves.
For if the stacked cords
speak of felled trees, of countless
five-foot logs flipped end over end downhill
till the blood is wrung from your back
and snowbound warmth must seem
so far off you would rather freeze,

yet each thin tongue torn from the grain
when log-halves were sundered at one stroke
will sing in the stove.
To remind you of hands. Of how
mere touch is song in the silence
where hands live — the song of muddy bark,

the song of sawdust like cornmeal and down,
and the song of one hand over another,
two of us holding the last length of the log
in the sawbuck as inches away the chainsaw
keeps ripping through hickory.

for Maxine Kumin

At Noon

The thick-walled room's cave-darkness,
cool in summer, soothes
by saying, This is the truth, not the taut
cicada-strummed daylight.
Rest here, out of the flame — the thick air's
stirred by the fan's four
slow-moving spoons; under the house the stone
has its feet in deep water.
Outside, even the sun god, dressed in this life
as a lizard, abruptly rises
on stiff legs and descends blasé toward the shadows.

The Cedar River

You bring the Dardevle back fast,
left wrist whirling in a circle
as the line fills the reel —
back from the water near reeds
where at the end of a long arc
it hit with a pop and leapt toward you.
It zags, jerks, darts, describes
a progress so quick
no nerves could catch it. Then
a tail-swirl riffles the surface . . .
and another pass, so high
the fins break through.
The marauding head —
eyes as low as the long jaw
that will snap sideways out of what
seems pure spite — rushes up
but the shape of the canoe
clouds its heaven and it panics.
The big splash of the escape
comes over the gunwale
and the lure hangs in its wake,
teasing the delicate tip of the rod
that nods like an innocent stalk of wild rice.

for Mark Haverland

Hoppy

Ancientest of cats, truest
model of decrepitude,
you shamble and push your own
sloppy shape across the room,
nosing the floor in your slow
unhappy step-by-step, and
with dollops of baby food
splashed around your whiskers, on
chin, on snout, and in one scarred
ear, don't you think it's gotten
crappy, this life, now the years
have slipped by, old Counselor?
You mop the rug with your tail,
you slap a tired paw against
the door, and turn dim yellow
eyes, flecked with a weariness
of having seen so much, back
over your jutting shoulder
to the faces that study
the exquisite mishap or
the dopey luck that has left
it to you — of all the world's
mopes and most unlikely wise,
prophets and poets — to stop
the bored chatter of these frail
merely human types and top
all their tiny, much-boasted
perseverances with your
pained, apocalyptic glance.

Dinokratous Street, Athens

On the half-shaded floor of the balcony
the sunlight bubbles like acid,
a year's dust frothing in the glare.
The morning was spent too near thrones
and the emptiness seeped into everyone,
everyone asleep now but me . . .

      so we have a reprieve
      from traveler's pique, from fear,
      from hurting and being hurt.

Below, in the city, there must be
some who watch over closed shops
and some who carry tea trays to rickety
tables that rock under elbows,
and some shoveling the brittle earth
of ruins into catch-screens
where something is always caught;
and some, barbarous and half-clothed,
scuff thirstily through the Agorá
where the thunder nearby is only the subway.

      The pepper-tree shade seethes in a swarm
      of winged shadows on the table tops,
      stirred by the breeze like a soundless hive.

Car horns honking in the rush, around
foreign mobs in bars and colonnades,
echo into dim sidestreets and dives
where coffee's a dollar a glass,
into the days that rot in a heart-pit of dreams —
of Chicago, New York, a Chevrolet,

and after years, a flush homecoming alongside
the tourists and diggers crowding the rail . . .

    Where the guides drive their groups
    against glass cases for a glimpse of ivory
    and gold, someone swears never to forgive.

And while my five friends have slept heavily
inside, weakened by their attention
to what's strange to us, new speech and eyes,
as we try to keep loving each other,
the shadow line has crept
across the threshing floor, opening
the air to the low sun, the slow slow crush
of the heat. And dreams and fears,
caught in the wind that
bursts up from the sea, blow away,
and the light falls down, burning
the stone and cement with its liquid weight.

    The lull before noise and night-hours.
    Listen:
    (Nikos said, "The Greeks hate silence.")

The Ruined Motel

Give the mourning doves any sun
at all and they will begin to grieve.
Their song, riding the steam that poured up
from the snow on the window-ledge,
came in to us as we scanned
the damp wreck of a seaside room,
all the things no one inherited:
the sour pink and beige paint,
a throng of water-stain shapes
on the walls — splotchy heads
and moldy animal herds — and behind us
brown vines leaning in at the door
to greet the webs and frost-burnt
mushrooms in the closet.

We sheltered there while our car
held alone the whole weedy expanse
of asphalt fronting the ocean,
and we listened to the cold wind
spill through the sea-grove and splash
against the line of downed carports
and the crowd of pines in the pool.

Looming ahead of us
at the end of the empty road, the shell
of the place had made us think
that it must have been ugly
even when new. Maybe ruined
it suits the small outpost of worshippers
nearby at Immanuel Baptist Church
(Fundamental and Independent)
who grasp their tradition with such force

they tear it apart, their fierce
conviction shredding the creeds
while doves coo and with a useless hiss
the sea bites into the beach-snow
and falls back across the crescent sands.

I was thinking, This was where we had brought
the nation, to neighboring new tries
either abandoned or shuddering inward with extremes —
till you said to me, The ghosts in this place
are unhappy. Then I too could hear them —
couples revenging the hours they had
together under ceilings
that never fell on them, the too-loud talk
at dinner and the hedging, hopeful
postcards in the morning.
We stepped away from them, from the boards
and slats of their collapsed beds,
from their fatigue, from musty air and dead wires,
we went back into the salt wind
and the noisy swaying pines, out
of that heap of winter-storm
tide-wrack. We didn't want to make
any mistakes but those we could say were ours.

But in that time we stayed there
we took the loss into ourselves,
obsessed with it — not stones
but rotting beaverboard and cold snake-nests,
not columns but dark hallways half-floored with sand.
And if the light that fell on us
as we walked toward the water,

that warmed our bones and stirred the doves,
made the scene seem a lesson-book —
the angles of human spaces, the path
upward — what did we read?
Under light-shafts from broken clouds,
an immense illumination
of breached walls, frail trees,
a narrow road, snow on the dunes,
dry weed-wisps and bright bits of plastic . . .
and rolling in the waves
like heads that strove
against their own deformity
the great whelks
dashed and battered till hope
was the hollowness in their cold clean skulls.

Prayer Before Bathing

Meat-fetor of a dog's breath;
the *tristeza* of a striptease;
an old man's gurgling rattling cough
that shakes him so wildly
he holds his sides and walks
in step with his convulsions
till they cease and he spits
on the sidewalk; blood
and gold dust on gauze
under the patient's hand,
where a surgeon had to cut
her ring away from the wound;
the old woman who sees the clock
reading 2:05 and in a little
girl's voice, a singing voice,
says loudly, "It's exactly
two o'clock!" and looks around
the room for an answer;
and every hope,
every book, ends with money;
and they say that the terror
in fairy tales is good for you;
and the priest walks slowly
across his campus and bends to pick up
each bit of stray paper and trash
on the path till with delicate
resignation he drops
his handful into a barrel;
and after the census,
when they take our names from us,
we must wash.

Those Who Are Gone

Have I betrayed your memory?
                              How many times!
The days pour down in a river, and a few trim boats,
well-used to work and cared-for well, float toward sea
alongside green slime and wrack in the muddy dregs.
If storms have drummed the banks upstream
more ruin descends — the water heaves and drags
its spoils under thumping ash-gray clouds
that flash with thrusting fire.
I say nothing, I offer no excuse. But other waters
rise silently from springs, drop by drop, seep up
from an unfathomable source to brim rock troughs,
then spill from crags and pinnacles, and thud
and burst and rush beneath the blue,
over clean stone. Those waters call your names forever.

                              after Antonio Machado

At the Temple
of Asklepios on Kos

At the Temple of Asklepios on Kos

Climbing toward the ancient source
while weighted down with injury —
one twisted ankle, some sunburn,
sulks, bad bowels, bruised
feelings — we felt pains
spark up our bones like
the flames that rise along a fuse.

No sign of snake or cock,
so we carried our thirst
far uphill to the tall
stone tub where the bees
swung back and forth at the spout,
following the smooth spill
to the ground,

and one of our countrymen,
not knowing how the spirit led him,
heaved himself up over
the high lip with a laugh
and dunked
his dirty head, fouling
the water for others.

We sipped nevertheless, sweet
taste, and started
up the wide staircase to the top,
my tongue rolling a cool word
in my mouth till I made
the connection: my work is to make,
to make speech whole, to heal.

Concerning the type

The poems of *The Ruined Motel* were set in linotype Electra, designed in the 1930s for the Mergenthaler Linotype Company by the American book and type designer William Addison Dwiggins. Electra is notably uniform in color, sharp and vibrant on the page. Its italic is unusual in being an oblique roman, a characteristic it shares with the display type, hand-set Perpetua italic. This highly recognizable face with many unusual elements was developed in the 1920s by the English stonecutter and calligrapher Eric Gill from his hand-carved letters.

Both faces, Electra and Perpetua, reflect the hand lettering of the artists behind them, two men of wide-ranging interests and talents.

Composition by American–Stratford Graphic Services, Inc.
Printing and binding by American Book – Stratford Press